MOMENTARY TURMOIL

ROBIN THOMAS

INDEPENDENT INNOVATIVE INTERNATIONAL

Published by Cinnamon Press
Meirion House
Tanygrisiau
Blaenau Ffestiniog
Gwynedd, LL41 3SU
www.cinnamonpress.com

ISBN: 978-1-78864-007-7

British Library Cataloguing in Publication Data. A CIP record for this book can be obtained from the British Library.

Designed and typeset in Palatino by Cinnamon Press. Printed in Poland.

Cover design by Adam Craig.

Cinnamon Press is represented in the UK by Inpress Ltd and in Wales by the Welsh Books Council.

Acknowledgements

Thanks to my many friends on the Reading poetry scene and to Todd Swift, Jan Fortune and Adam Craig for their support, advice and encouragement.

Thanks are also due to the editors of the following, in which some of these poems previously appeared:
Agenda, Envoi, Orbis, Brittle Star, Pennine Platform, The High Window, Poetry Scotland, South, Poetry Salzburg Review, Stand and the University of Reading *Creative Arts Anthology.*

Contents

Bright Yarn   9
Cafferty's Truck   10
Sun-Dappled Garden   11
Max Ament   12
Train Landscape   13
A, G, B to E and, Oh Dear, F   14
Theme and Variations   16
Miles Ahead   18
Short Nature   20
Dzhaz   21
Expedition   22
Tarascon Stagecoach   23
Les Sables d'Olonne   24
High Heels   25
De Aanslag (Amsterdam 1943)   26
Convoy Duty 1943   27
Neighbours   28
Froxfield Stop Off   30
The Toper   31
Portrait Of Giovanni Della Volta
        With His Wife And Children   32
Straight From The Oven   33
Villiers Street – Dusk   34
The Girl from Ipanema and
        'an Interesting Bunch of Guys'   35
Swing, Brother, Swing   36
A Short History Of Falmouth   38
Curtains   39
Mist   40
Pigeon   41
Right and Wrong   42
Giovanni Agostino and His Son Niccola   43
Francesco Albani   44
Grasped   45
How Annoying Gravity Is   46
And These, Gentlemen   48
River   49
Event   50
John Evelyn's Voyage to Italy   51
Excursion   52

Christ Taking Leave of his Mother   53
Lunchtime   54
Wind in the Willows   56
Feline Ontology   57
Last Train   58
Postcard   59
It Still Returns   60
Sunday   61

For Mary and Caitlin

Momentary Turmoil

Bright Yarn

The yarn of bright wool snaking across Great Aunt Edith's bed where she was propped up knitting socks for me and dying for herself was like the road snaking through the Chilterns to Henley where duty would take us weekly to sit in her dim, tiny room heaped with the smell of sickness. Returning into the night we would turn off the main road and into what seemed like a darkroom, made so by the tall darkness of trees, our headlights making little impression. Once as we slowed we saw an adult and two young deer. They looked at us, motionless, expressionless, as if trying to fix our image. The road home from there was a half-seen promontory in a sea of shadows, an argument where there is no giving way.

Cafferty's Truck

Cafferty's rackety truck brings the sad news
as gulls wheel and screech
over the small, grey town.

Cafferty stops at each house.
Gulls shriek their senseless fugue.
The town gets smaller, greyer.

Cafferty's done. The gulls' eyes glitter.
They criss-cross the sky, bickering, snatching.
The town settles and sighs.

Byrne, in his trim red van,
respectfully follows
Cafferty's yesterdays with his tomorrows.

Sun-Dappled Garden

The garden unfurls like a sandy beach,
the waves are fondling, fondling, fondling.
Edward, stay back, don't go in so deep.

The sharks are circling the apple tree.
There's young life to smell, blood on their lips,
their jaws long to grip, their bodies convulse.

Edward, I beg you, don't take a chance.
'Come to me, come', say the finny enticers.
Edward, oh Edward, stand tall, be yourself,

not meat for the satans sardonically circling.
Remain in the sun-dappled garden with me.

Max Ament

Max Ament was born in 7th District, Vienna, on September 9th 1933, the youngest of five children from a prosperous family of lawyers and entrepreneurs. Showing early prowess in music, he entered the Vienna Conservatory at the age of fifteen where he studied conducting under Hans Swarowsky and composition with Joseph Marx. While still at the Conservatory, he conducted his double concerto for oboe and bassoon at the Vienna Musikverein to instant acclaim and he was thereafter able to support himself full time as a composer.

In his long career he produced a large body of work, including five operas, three large-scale choral works, four symphonies, five string quartets, three piano sonatas; concertos and concertante works, song cycles and incidental music. The works for which he is best known are the Cello Concerto, the oratorio *Ein Kind Unserer Zeit* and in particular his opera sequence: *Die Reise, Der Kommandant* and *Der Schwarze Hund.*

He leaves a widow, Anna, and four sons: Erich, a specialist in European jurisprudence at the International Court of Justice, The Hague; Anton, Professor of moral philosophy at Princeton University, New Jersey; David, a noted novelist and poet and Baruch, leader of the Social Democratic party of Austria.

Max Ament

Born 1933 Vienna, died 1943 Belsen

Train Landscape

Eric Ravilious, 1939

Why, Eric? Why is this
meticulously clean, oak-faced,
horsehair-stuffed, leather-strapped,
old-fashioned third-class
railway compartment
motionless? Why is it
here under Westbury Hill,
its famous white horse
framed by the left hand window?
And why is it empty?

The brim of his blue sun hat
almost in contact,
a small bent man
in a sleeveless jacket
intervenes and peers.
Closer, closer. If only
he could get close enough.

A, G, B to E and, Oh Dear, F

Quiet Carriage

Passengers are reminded
that we have two quiet carriages:
A in standard, G in first,
where you are asked
not to use mobile phones
or stereo equipment
and to keep noise to a minimum.
Also, in coach G,
you are requested to speak in whispers,
not to eat crisps, nuts, sandwiches or hamburgers
or indeed anything which can be purchased from the buffet car.
Sandwiches of thinly sliced wild organic pacific salmon
are an exception. You are further requested
not to remove outer clothing
unless you have used deodorant.
Do not sniff. Do not slurp drinks.
Do not read the *Daily Mail*
unless it is disguised with brown paper.
Do not speak at all if you have a northern accent.

Loud Carriage

Passengers are reminded
that we have four loud carriages,
B to E, where you are expected
to cough, sniff and scrunch paper bags,
to talk as loudly as you can and hoot with laughter
at jokes which are devoid of humour.
You should bellow into mobile phones,
shouting details of your divorce,
or why Harry, sitting two seats away,
has to be sacked
or that you are on the train.

If you are quiet in any loud carriage
you will be asked to transfer
to the punishment carriage, F,
where, unless you recant,
you will be required
to write an essay in which are elucidated
the provisions of Magna Carta,
write a villanelle in Latin
and/or compile a report
on the recent downturn
in sales of guttering in Lithuania.

Theme and Variations

An Experiment on a Bird in the Air Pump — Joseph Wright of Derby, 1768

The White Cockatoo

The scientist looks
not at his apparatus but into a distance.
A seated man peers at the table. Another
examines an empty cage. A boy
cannot take his eyes off the dying bird, a second
interrupts his work to glance into
some other distance. Lovers gaze at each other.
'Listen, watch, learn' says a kindly-stern father.
His daughters look away. The moon looks down.

The Pump

The scientist who sucks out the bird's life
stares at the future. The small girls
in white dresses cannot be consoled.
The moon, pale, silent, sucks the life
out of the colours. The lovers oblivious,
the moon oblivious, the girls
heartbroken. The lovers,
the moon, the pump,
the silence.

The Moon

the scientist stares
a man looks away
a boy observes
a man considers
a boy wonders
a father points
the girls cannot look
a lover looks
at a lover looks
at a lover
the moon pales
the girls cry
the bird dies

Miles Ahead

I. Here Come De Honey Man

Miles at his shoulder, leaning,
pointing. Bill's fingers
stretched, overlapped, searching.

eggshell sounds, hovering silences
a sea of surging chords

Man, cool it, we don't want no white opinions.

Stops his stream of sound, turns,
summons from Evans those
crystal notes cascading down a waterfall.

II. Move

Inspected by a very reliable contact. Described as straight inner
structure and inner fender panels. Good body gaps and panel fit. US
delivery. New to Miles Davis.

Do not get out of your car.
Get your license, registration and insurance papers out and ready.

Move slowly and deliberately.

Miles pulling alongside the Bentley, calling, hoarse: *Want to race?*

What are you doing with this car?

III. Gone

he signals
the cab pulls up
he kisses her pale cheek
What! Mist. Swirl. Red.
Copped.

The Miura came apart like Brazilian plywood in the rain.
I grabbed the bags and ran to the sewer. He screamed,
What the fuck you doing?
Miles got real quiet: I always wondered
who that white mother fucker was.
You thank him for me, and tell him to come by anytime.

IV. It Ain't Necessarily So

cosmic labyrinths
                    fractured, piercing, broken
grandiose dissonance
                    darting, dancing
Arabic scales, African, Spanish
                 rubato howl

My best friend is Gil Evans.

Notes:
Bill Evans was the pianist in Miles Davis's quintet in the late 1950s. *Gil* Evans was the composer, arranger and band leader with whom Davis collaborated from time to time in concerts and in the studio.

The Lamborghini Miura was one of a series of outrageously powerful sports cars owned by Davis.

Short Nature

The train is stuck, the driver
cannot be found.
Someone
is going to be very sorry.

The ten-o-six service,
we are sorry to announce,
has been delayed. This is due to
an obstruction on the line.

If, due to the short nature of some platforms,
passengers at affected stations
do not alight from the middle carriage,
they will be sorry.

The train is stuck.
There is no driver, only obstruction
and short platforms,
which is a pity.

The train will not stop.
The driver cannot be prevailed upon.
There is no obstruction, no delay,
and no pity.

Due to the short nature
of the journey, passengers are advised
not to invest too much in it, otherwise
they will be sorry.

Due to the shortness of nature
passengers are advised
not to invest too much in the journey.
We are sorry.

Dzhaz

Leningrad, 1928

Waltz
Polka
Foxtrot for Symphony Orchestra -
Shostakovich Opus 16

Moscow, 1936

The editorial board of *Pravda*,
endorsing jazz, hurls Molotov cocktails
at that of *Izvestia*, which, denouncing it,
bombards the *Pravda* board
likewise with ordinance. *The Truth*
prevails. Each board member
of *Reports of Soviets*
of Peoples' Deputies of the USSR
receives a pre-dawn visit.

Minsk, 1940

Adolph Ignatievich (Eddie) Rosner ,
late of Weintraub's Syncopators of Berlin,
recognising that 'it didn't help
being a Jew playing Negro music
even if your name is Adolf'
joins the State Jazz Orchestra
of the Byelorussian Soviet Republic.

Baku, 1953

No city
in the Union of Soviet Socialist Republics
'is more receptive to hard bop
(jazz is outlawed, Rosner in Siberia)
than the capital city of Azerbaijan'.

Expedition

Great God! This is an awful place —Captain Scott

Several times a day my mother
sets out for the South Pole:
struggles layer by layer into outdoor gear
tugs at her snow boots, threads and tightens laces
comes blinking out of her tent
loads the sled, calms the leaping, yapping huskies
inches forward into the wind.

At night she eyes the mountain
readies herself with ropes, crampons, grappling gear, pitons
hauls herself up
reaches the summit with a great sigh
stares into the unfathomable dark.

Tarascon Stagecoach

How could it be? It was
'lost and forlorn' in an
African desert, he'd
read in *Tartarine*,

yet it's here, in Arles,
looking tidy enough,
in red and dark green,
its wheel rims
fresh painted in cream,

but awry, tipped back,
as if near the top
of a hill. There's a ladder
for luggage, or
maybe a prop, preventing
its slide on the seasick paint
—grey, blue and white—
into a fury of yellow.

Alphonse Daudet, *Tartarin de Tarascon,* 1872; Vincent van Gogh, *The Tarascon Stagecoach,* October 1888. Van Gogh cut off his ear in December of that year.

Les Sables d'Olonne

Albert Marquet (1921)

The air, the water,
a bilious continuum.
Houses a string
of parched skulls.
In the distance
a town, indefinite
except for its church.
Against the quay
a three master
declines into its past.

Tilting in the thick air,
the treacly water, boats
blatantly smuggle:
muddy fields, cow pats,
sea-weed, duck eggs,
fresh-sliced beetroot,
day old mustard.

High Heels

Women! Don't you like men?
Because why do you wear high heels,
plaster yourselves with mud,
thin yourselves to a slice of lettuce
leaving men in an ecstasy of indifference?
And men, what about you? Why
would you stick your noses up your friends' bums
in the febrile mud, unite in exclusive drunkenness,
jump up and down on glass floors?
Come on men! Plaster your faces with orange poison!
Totter around on nine-inch heels!
Show some solidarity! And women,
scrape off that muck, get yourselves floppy sweaters,
brew yourselves a cup of tea,
get stamp-collecting!

De Aanslag (Amsterdam 1943)

i.m. Harry Mulisch

Laat de hond alleen!
shouts young Harry
but the red faced milkman
whose dog it is
swings his great fist,
knocks him to the ground,
Gut gemacht, Junge
says the man who helps him up
an officer in black.

Convoy Duty 1943

They wear duffel coats, peaked caps,
towels for scarves.

Enters the blue-green and white
wave-hill. Down, down
and up, shaking itself
like a wet dog.

They watch through binoculars for death,
hoping for life.

Hurls itself forward,
burrowing into the wave-ridge,
smashing it
to glittering fragments.

Down, down,
up.

Neighbours

i.m. Miep Gies

Brown beans, split peas, potatoes,
turnip tops, newspapers,
underwear, soap, candles,
meat in the early days, later,
blood sausage; a belt, books
from the library, oats,
handkerchiefs, sweet peas,
peonies, kale, cigarettes,
sauerkraut, yoghurt, jam, biscuits,
film magazines, exercise books,
flour, and for birthdays:
sweets, full cream cheese,
beer, lemon syrup, spice cake,
piccalilli, treacle and once:
vintage wine.

You, Miep, shopped, bartered, stole
and carried all these by hand
down cold streets, past nervous,
quizzical, grey-uniformed boys,
and entered the building,
the Luger, the twisted face
a routine peril. There you shared
outside news, jokes, brought fresh air,
day after day, month after month.

Afterwards you went back
Into that echoing building,
the pistol, the contorted face
in every creak, every shadow.
But you climbed the stairs, went in,
collected her scattered papers.

The day the radio told of your death,
snow lay round our cosy house,
much as it must have done
round Anne's shivering hut as she lay dying.
Our neighbours worked for hours to create
a huge snowman. Next morning
their children rushed out to see it
but its head was gone, its body spoilt.
I helped them repair it. There's some merit,
isn't there, Miep, in that?

Froxfield Stop Off

I'm alone in the lounge of the Bull's Head,
sipping tea. The only sound is of cars
accelerating on the long sweep of road
out of Froxfield, whose 'bracken and blackberry,
harebell and dwarf gorse' the drivers won't see.
Edward Thomas was here the year
my mother was born, writing about time,
not knowing how little remained. Today
I sold her flat while she continues to wonder
—does she?—whether to stay in it. Bit by bit
I am signing her away. I finish my tea, walk
across the car park, switch my phone back on.

The Toper

Ferdinand Bol 1650-51, (The Wallace Collection)

It's hard, so hard.
Coming here, will it help?

These dusty cabinets,
this endless stream
of dead life.
This empty armour. Think
of the men who wore it:
the clang of death,
the jolting litters,
last drops of wine
eased between grateful lips.

Can't think of that.
What's this? A
florid kind of bowl,
Wine cooler. Urbino. 1560.
You'd see these nymphs
swaying under the cool water,
bottles resting pert,
awaiting your pleasure.

No. Move on.
Who's this big Dutchman?
'Ja, zo, now you kom!
You are behint. I
haf been drinking for two!
Here, take!'

Portrait Of Giovanni Della Volta
With His Wife And Children

Lorenzo Lotto 1547

Twenty ducats!

Sit there please and there.
Madam, Your Excellency,
your charming children there.

For your expression, I must ask you *(again)*
to look at me.   *You won't? You'll gaze in
ennui into some imaginary place?   I'll
do my best.*

                *That ought to do it. Enough
to break the paint I think.*   Yes the children,
reach for cherries, of course.

Fifty ducats, no, not a joke.
Signore, please.

Straight From The Oven,

the cake,
his mother presenting it proudly,
his father holding him up to see.
He, without warning,
plunging his finger into its core.

This one, look,
You can still see the scar, just.

His father is gone now,
his mother is frail.
Will their love warm him as he grows old?
Will the scar still be there
when he slides into the oven?

Villiers Street—Dusk

light darks
the river invisibles
hurriers clack
drinkers bulge
cobbles slime
news flaps
windows gloat
she will not come
she will not come

The Girl from Ipanema
and 'an Interesting Bunch of Guys'

Stan's waving a gun. He
smacks her in the face, their daughter
screaming. He's after money,
for 'stuff'.

João's never there, he's
with the black dog, he's
put away, he's out again. It's
always there: thirty times
they try to get it right,
the 'o' in 'rosa'.

Astrud's come with husband João,
sings it around the place. *I want her
on the disc* says Stan, *No*
says Joao, *Yes* says Stan,
Yes she says to Stan,
Not any more to João.

Gentle strokes draw out the samba,
floats and sways serene and gentle
and when Stan breathes
each one who hears it
goes *aaah*. Oh,
but it isn't just beauty
in the gossamer sound they create,
but Stan doesn't know what it is
and João doesn't know what it is
and Astrud, who wants to know, doesn't
for nobody knows what it is.

Swing, Brother, Swing

i.m. Benny Goodman and Fletcher Henderson

1. The Palomar Ballroom

They're lost in mid-America,
the money, the illusions
draining in endless drives
through flickering nights. There's
one more night and one more chance,
at the Palomar, Hollywood. Sweet music,
dance tunes out of Guy Lombardo:
the air thick with indifference,
the dancers want home.
We're going nowhere, Benny,
Let's play our own thing, might as well
and Swing begins.

(Black chemists not required,
black music yes, so Henderson
makes a living. His band swings
from the first, can't stop itself)

2. The Big Broadcast

Ida, sweet as apple cider,
Avalon, Can't give you
anything but love. Rosetta,
Chloe, Tea for two. Rajah
of Rhythm, King of Swing.

(Henderson does ok,
in Harlem, through 1929,
then it's harder, no Palomar
for him. Goodman
buys his music, buys his time,
buys him, body and soul)

3. Carnegie Hall

Round block stretching, buzzing, almost
jitterbugging through the doors. Nothing
so modern ever, ditching Mozart, ditching
Mom and apple pie.

Goodman thoughtful, fluent, mournful,
floats above the big hits, then,
as the band switches mode,
weaves himself into the Henderson sound:
the supple pulse, the chanting brass, the choir of reeds.

A Short History Of Falmouth

White flash swirl in shout of wind
over buckle of boats' ugly dance,
window drums behind
dam of files, boxes,
newspapers, manifests shielding
an intent, patient man
in the Cornwall records office
who is herding the past -
charter, Custom House,
packet station, docks, mutinies,
Trafalgar, railways, Campbeltown,
Overlord, decline -
into the pages of a book
to be perfect-bound, shelved.

Curtains

Seeing a great shadow
pass across the window,
Mrs Simpkins moved the curtain
just enough to peep out.
What she saw was
Tyrannosaurus Rex
becoming extinct.

Mist

The mist is everywhere, thieving colour,
cramping the sun, converting trees into
clawing aggressors. It presses on the car,
my solitude. A dance of half-lights seen ahead
offers meagre comfort—I'll keep in touch, no,
gone. It lifts for a moment. What's this?
My father's face is white, my mother's wet.
What had I done? Behind, a shape appears
with seething lights—*there is no mist for me*—
and sweeps past, hurtles into its future.

Pigeon

head pop
back pop front
underfoot
gets what nothing
else dares
all stomach
pecks
what nothing
else will
leaves
unscrubbable
moulded multi-
hued calling
card *will come again*
magics same
size young join
squabbles of
marauding pirates which
disturbed
scatter-clattering-flap

normally winners
head pop back
pop front
under paused traffic-
light-tyre looking
for ... but
sometimes not

Right and Wrong

Nurse, one of the twins
will not survive the night.
Please separate them.

the doctor is right
or probably right
or possibly right
or wrong but
the nurse has no right
to think herself right
she might do great wrong

but the nurse is right
to think herself right
thank god for the nurse
who is right to be wrong

Giovanni Agostino and His Son Niccola

Lorenzo Lotto 1515

Turned from a busy desk, book in hand, the elder
peers at me. He thinks
I don't believe in God and holds the proof,
his finger in the exact place.

At his shoulder stands his son—larger, pinker,
bearded, blacker cloak, bigger hat.
He likes me! He wants to be my friend.
I think he'd like my house.

Francesco Albani

Giovanni Cariani 1517

Look then,
but acknowledge
that to permit you sight of me
is condescension
beyond the ordinary.

Step back and take me in. Attend to
this great sweep of tooled gold
with its touches of smalt, vermillion
which I seem to wear.
Observe this glowing mix
of malachite, verdigris, green earth—
plain to the left, figured to the right -
as if it were a curtain.

And then the area
you could call my face -
note how it balances the rest.

Grasped

Cro-Magnon man's handaxe would fit
if you could extract it through the glass
snug in your palm.

You can imagine this carp's tongue sword
balancing in your hand
its blade ready.

To lie in state among helmets, rings
caskets, necklaces, sceptres
bracelets, drinking horns, ingots,
is not so different from your being here.

A plumber's screwdriver is poking
through his ancient bag. He ignores
the beckoning cabinets and goes
about his business in the hidden places.

Go home and find a screwdriver.
Feel its smooth handle, insert it
into the groove on a screw's head.
Feel the joy of its turning.
Be that plumber.

How Annoying Gravity Is

The plate drops and smashes, the jar falls
and mixed nuts or tomato ketchup cover the floor
or I am dashed to pieces on the rocks below.

Every time I try to keep something up—a radio,
myself in January, a just hatched chick, the cat
licking its lips below, down it goes.

At other times, mind you, gravity's great.
Imagine diving into a swimming pool without it
or if it suddenly evaporated in mid air. Imagine
trying to make a sandwich or lay a carpet or drive to the shops.

But still, what if I didn't want dispersed matter
to coalesce all the bloody time? Or if I was prepared to put up with
most of the macroscopic objects in the universe not existing
at least some of the space-time?

I'd have to switch off one of the four fundamental interactions of
                                                            nature
(the others are animal magnetism, the strong force—
the Russian army waiting to cross the Oder in March '45
is a good example, the weak one—my backhand).

What would be really handy would be
to be able to switch mass on and off as it suited me—off
as the marmite spread slice hurtled sod's law-wise towards the
white carpet—on as I poured Belgian beer into a glass on a warm
summer's day—of course, I'd have to be very careful how I did it.

Notes:

1. *Laika,* literally *Barker,* became the first animal to orbit the earth in 1954

2. *Animal magnetism* (French: *magnétisme animal;* Latin: *magnetismus animalis*) is a term proposed by Franz Mesmer in the 18th century, the term 'magnetism' was adopted by analogy, referring to some interpersonal and general effects of reciprocal influence and/or entanglement he observed.

3. As World War II went on, the complement of supporting units attached to a Soviet army became larger and more complex. By 1945, a Soviet army typically had attached mortar, antitank, anti-aircraft, howitzer, gun–howitzer, rocket launcher, independent tank, self-propelled gun, armored train, flamethrower, and engineer-sapper units.

4. Can anyone help me with my backhand?

And these, Gentlemen,

are from planet 'Earth'. Did you know
that they are mortal and aware of it?
That's why, we think, they kill.
And also why,
bizarre phenomenon,
they so love to acquire things -
brutal acceptance, deep denial.
Also, they make pictures of themselves,
the enduring and the transient
strangely combined.
I have one of their images here:
this is a naked male and these are arrows.
Attractive, isn't it?

River

Outside the home
where my mother is waited on,
is waiting patiently,
the polished green-brown river
has stopped, but somehow feeds the weir
which sparkles and hisses
into momentary turmoil.

Event

he sits on the chair
he crosses his legs
he opens the newspaper
the cat jumps up
she brings him tea
he asks her
she says
the cat jumps down
he stands
throws the chair
through the window

John Evelyn's Voyage to Italy

Outward from Cannes, bound for Genoa,
weather fine, weather fine,
waves pendulous, mirroring, scattering,

choppy, increasing, darkening,
black, rocking, tilts, crash
of wave, of ship,
timbers grind, spars
shift, sea
bubbles, surging in, traders,
sailors, wives, monks,
children, Evelyn, a bishop
bail.
Captain implores,
shouted confessions
lost in the shriek, in
hurls of sea and

gone, the shocked boat
rocking, exhausted, as, rolling in
from an invisible shore, a scent
in which might perfectly be smelt
the peculiar joys of Italy:
orange, citron and jasmine,
for divers leagues to seaward

Excursion

I'm through the Gallery doors, heading
for *L'allée à Chantilly* which I enter
to find myself under its frondescent canopy.
The river is leaf-painted emerald as I slip
in and down, down, through blue-green,
cobalt, indigo, glittering shoals, inquisitive
shadows, towering, sunken,
a huge ocean liner, here for eternity,
home for viperfish, fangtooth, coffinfish, squid
and I'm strolling under chandeliers,
the deck shifting softly, the fans, the waiters,
the tie-loosening warmth and out
through portholed doors and into the
Gallery, to gaze at Cezanne's
L'allée à Chantilly.

Christ Taking Leave of his Mother

Wolf Huber, about 1520

Grief in every face, every posture, garment,
grief condensing in the dim light, dripping from trees,
suffusing her body,
collapsing her face,
softening her bones.

The women, drained, grey,
are altogether with her,
their support vital, futile.

Only His hands are seen, blessing His mother
as all men bless their mothers
as all men take their leave of their mothers.

Lunchtime

after Frank O'Hara

I'm wishing I could see
the hum-colored cabs and
the waterfall and stop
for a cheeseburger at
JULIET'S CORNER
and chocolate malted
          but
it's 12 o'clock in Caversham
where the sky is always grey
and the precinct's always dirty
and the facias
have not been cleaned
for more than fifty years and
Marc Antoni is scowling at
a crouching Chrystal Dragon
and nails bespeak and Lily Ink
tattoos and you can, if you want,
Go Sing in the N W TES
AMENT CHURCH OF GOD
          and
I've time to nip across to
Waitrose for a sandwich,
past the girl selling a
Big Issue
and I'm in Aladdin's larder
where there's
oranges, organic, and avocados,
apples and brown bread in
baskets and chicken, cheap
or chic, farmed, free-range and
fresh, and vegetables,
vast volumes of fish
on ice, silvery, slithery, starey,
          where
thimblefuls of wine are offered
to the faithful, where sausages

are regal and biscuits
raise a royal hand, where aisle-rage
is rare and there are magazines
you'd never buy to
while away the time you're
in the queue and
I've got my sushi now and I'm out
into the freshness
of the car park with
Lunch Poems in my pocket.

Wind in the Willows

and another thing
that happened:
as I turned,
my coat, which I hadn't yet taken off
clipped Toad of Toad Hall,
one of the Royal Doulton
Wind in the Willows collection
which we had bought
from the antique shop
in Goring earlier that year

Feline Ontology

I pull the damp clothes out
and into the basket, pick up the bag of pegs,
carry it all through the French windows.

Today, the garden is a bath of warmth and light,
an enclosure assembled from
as many shades of spring fresh green
as you can think of.   As I hang out the clothes
God sends a cat which
mews in greeting, rolls on its back,
invites me to stroke its soft fur.

'The bastard! He doesn't exist!'
said Beckett, but I
must praise that Being which exists
or not, according to its will.

Last Train

Eschewing vistas
windows image
swaying tableaux -
floating shadows
pallid chamber
folded bodies
not the river
black below.

Postcard

On the front of this postcard you will see mountains covered in snow. I can see them from the window in my room, which is tiny and the shower doesn't work. The breakfast is all yoghurt and soft cheese. On the first day the driver didn't know the way; luckily, Javad speaks Turkish which is a kind of lingua franca and we got there in the end. The boss is Dutch, he's here to be with his local family. The days are filled with milky coffee and partners arguing. In the evenings we go to Mad Murphys. Max keeps disappearing for secret meetings. Tomorrow we go up into the mountains for grilled meat and vodka. Best wishes for the wedding.

It still returns,

the ice-cream
my daughter,
aged five,
holding ready to eat,
by the sun green grass river sparkle,
lost hold of,
dropped.

If I could return to that time
and buy another,
and hold it for her,
she curling her small fingers round the cone,

I would.

Sunday

is marred
by foreboding

the valley casts
its long shadow

but the coming of Monday
or death

is probably
no big deal